Praise for *Multitude*

"Rich in ideas and agitational ends. The 'multitude' is Hardt and Negri's term for the earth's six billion increasingly networked citizens, an enormous potential force for 'the destruction of sovereignty in favor of democracy.' . . . Written for activists to provide a solid goal (with digressions into history and theory) toward which protest actions might move, this timely book brings together myriad loose strands of far left thinking with clarity, measured reasoning and humor, major accomplishments in and of themselves."

—*Publishers Weekly* (starred review)

"Impressive . . . a rare and exciting work of synthesis, this selection nicely blends some of the most cutting-edge scholarly work on globalization into a relatively accessible package."

—*Booklist* (starred review)

"Perhaps the most important piece of global analysis since Tariq Ali's *Clash of Fundamentalisms*."

—*Press Action*